SUSURRUS

Susurrus is the rustling of the sea,
Below the sandcliff, moving quietly;
And, as I write, I hear its wondrous sound.
The sibilance gives gentling to the heart
Should it be troubled in its loneliness,
And with its whisperings creates a part
Of a recurring stillness in the soul
That rules serene in its tranquillity.

J.B.G.

SUSURRUS

POEMS BY

Jane Baldwin Gillespie

William L. Bauhan, Publisher
DUBLIN, NEW HAMPSHIRE

Library of Congress Cataloguing in Publication Data:
Gillespie, Jane Baldwin, 1909-
Susurrus: poems / by Jane Baldwin Gillespie.
p. cm.
ISBN 0-87233-091-5
I. Title.
PS3557.I3792S87 1987 87-16829 CIP
811'54–dc19

This book was set in Palacio type by debset, Peterborough, N.H., printed at the Transcript Printing Company, Peterborough, and bound at the New Hampshire Bindery, Concord, N.H.

Printed in the United States of America

FOR

Jill and Vanessa

CONTENTS

Counterpoint 15
Early Light 16
Prayer 17
Moment of Light 18
Bay Ballet 19
Memorable Print 20
Wise Choice 1984 21
Sonnet of Love 22
Clarity 23
Learning 24
August Day 25
Reality 26
Free Flight 27
Spirit 28
Early Moon 29
Our Strength 30
Vapors 31
Full Moon and Clouds 32
Success? 33
Compliance 34
Serenity 35
Christmas 36
Change 37
Very Early Spring 38
Quiescence 39
Mutuality 40
My Sister Fan—1973 41
Mid-March 42
Our World 43
Erosion 44

A Fillip 45
Questing 46
Lustrous Day 47
Time Off 48
Violation – 1975 49
Refugees 50
Regeneration 51
Spaceship Earth 52
A Game of Checkers 53
January Jinks 54
Eclipse – May 30, 1984 55
Solitude 56
Submission 57
Young Moon 58
Development 59
Interim 60
Sorrow 61
Monotone 62
Vigilant 63
Venture 64
Communion 65
Light-ness 66
Living 67
Progression 68
Directions 69
Summer Sonnet 70
Warning of the Wind 71
Symbiosis 72
Offering 73
Meteorite – March 1983 74
Summer 1978 75
Blame 76
Twilight 77
Outlook 78

Accountability	79
The Cardinal	80
Thankfulness	82
A Small Star	83
Sunset Light	84
Windows on the World	85
Capability	86
Sonnet	87
Soul's Perspective	88
Restorative	89
Effort	90
Moon Frame	91
Share with Love	92
Complacency	93
Disparity	94
Faith	95

SUSURRUS

Counterpoint

The storm is over, and the weather breaks;
The sun appears in fleeting moment proud,
Emerging from the glory of a cloud;
The shadows on the water move along,
As more and bigger clouds arrive on range.
The intercepting rays of light emit
A radiance contrasting with the shade.
The wind is high and strong, thus making change
Of light and shadow on the ruffled bay,
A sweep of beauty in its varied way.
The shifting, diverse motions of the sea,
Reveal a studied continuity.
The silence of the water listening
And waiting for the windsong of the day
Divulges a relationship so true—
It counterpoints our harmony of two.

Early Light

The early morning sunlight on the bay
Has glints within its path more than the moon's;
The sparkling is so bright it makes my eyes
Close tight in sheer protection from the glare
But open right away to look again.
The many facets in the rippling waves
Of dancing sun rays glittering with joy,
Are soon hypnotic in their hold on me,
As I continue looking at them gleam.
Then glancing further I see mistiness
Across the bay and by the ocean's shore;
The light within that haze is mystical,
As if some saint, in deep serenity,
Is wondering, and wandering betimes.
I watch in fascination quite a while,
Convinced, as always, that the beauty shown
Is one of God's great gifts to earthlings now.

Prayer

Of what is man that Thou art mindful, Lord,
That Thou shouldst come to earth to visit him?
Thou gavest of Thyself to help blot out
Our selfishness and sins with all Thy love.
Help us, we pray, to love Thee as we should,
And act accordingly, in Christian faith.
Please make us know, particularly now—
In times of fear, of hardness, poverty—
Our souls are in Your Image, not our flesh,
And that we have to learn the difference.

Moment of Light

A rift in the grey-like nimbus,
Revealing cerulean blue,
A joyous and welcome spaceway
Inviting the light to come through.

A moment of brilliant color
On sandbars the essence of gold.
Emitting a special aura;
Ephemeral joy to behold.

It made me a part of something,
Of what it is hard to explain,
Except that for just one instant
Earth's innocence reached out again.

Bay Ballet

The bay is dancing in the sun,
Its glory like a thousand gems,
Its sparkling light is glittering
In fragments of scintilla grace.
And swallows swoop in blithe jeté
From off the sandcliff, in the air,
In imitation of ballet,
As if Baryshnikov were there.
It is a day that's just begun,
But through it all, in ecstasy,
I'll know increasingly the truth,
In finding beauty there is love.

Memorable Print

It's just before dark,
And everything's gray.
The water and sky
Give quite a display
Of quiet oneness,
With certain dismay
At the loneliness
Of what could be gay
In color and light.
But for the whole day
The very flat seascape
Has witnessed no ray
Of brightness anywhere.
It is hard to say
Where horizons end–
Sky with waterway.
But there is this, too,
In seeking a way
Quite indelible
To lure this to stay
In mind's memory,
I surely can say,
It's a Whistler print–
So vivid it may,
In retrospection
Become one today.

Wise Choice 1984

A Jew by birth is now a cardinal;
A fact deserving thought, that would appear
To be a stroke of genius that is clear
And utterly in keeping with the times.
How thrilling that this man is part of both
Judeo-Christian background and belief.
The inspiration of the pope was deep
To choose a priest with strength to coalesce
Religions that can help to unify
This frightened world of ours from sore distress.

Sonnet of Love

To love completely is a loveliness
That is a difficulty to convey;
For over everything it must portray
The very essence of true happiness.
This special love precludes all selfishness
That could usurp the heart, perhaps betray
The nature of itself with such dismay
It then might create undue bitterness.
To search for something that is hard to find
Takes patience with an overwhelming trust,
That first is all-inclusive in the mind,
Becoming active, knowing that it must
Eventually realize its goal
In knowing love within another's soul.

Clarity

No clouds today, the sky so clear
The azure mirrors in the sea,
As if to sense itself so near
It must perceive its brilliancy.
A single sailboat thwarts the tide,
Its whiteness seeming kerchief size,
As etched against the bluer side
It sleeks along in graceful guise.
While gulls in lilting mockery
Rasp sharply in staccato cries,
The gleaming sunlight's sorcery
Evokes the blueness of the skies.

Learning

We have so many problems to resolve;
Strategic arms, ecology, and wars,
Potential wars, too, ever cropping up,
And hunger, drugs, and how to help our youth;
A host of situations to be solved,
And worked out in a truly Christian way.
But that is why we're here—to learn to cope.
It seems to me that Earth is like a school
Where everyone is given each his chance
To prove himself as well as he can do,
But relative to what he starts out with—
Our limitations are well known by God,
He leaves it up to us to do our part,
To conquer not the world but just ourselves,
For strangely when we win the fight of self
Then we have won the world in doing so,
And in the victory, things mesh with ease.
The paradoxes in this life are great:
The more we give the more we have to give,
In loving we attain the gift of love,
And from our weaknesses there come our strengths,
The finding of one's self comes from the losing.
It's all a thrilling learning-process fine,
Wherein we grow to stature that is true,
For only each one's capabilities.
The Lord presents these challenges to us
To make a transformation in life's span.
Let's put our hands in God's and feel the light.

August Day

This is a lovely day the Lord has made,
So then must we rejoice and show our praise.
The beauty all about us nudges us
To fill our hearts with glory and delight;
To listen to the water's sibilance—
Susurrus sounds that offer inward peace.
The indigo of sea and sky combine
To complement the brilliancy of light,
As the horizon echoes softnesses
In lavender and pink against the green
Of hills along the island far away.
A few stray clouds compute the distances
Of land and water in a lovely blend
And seem to smile with shy benevolence
As I regard them in their quiet sphere.
It is a date to show our gratitude
For all the blessings given to enjoy,
As in our spirits we can realize
The plenitude of nature's graciousness
That God so freely offers for our joy.

Reality

Shadow, substance. What is meant?
Something reached for? Gained, then spent?
Shadows often create fear,
Substance though is strong and clear.
Hourly we must keep apart
Shadow, substance, in the heart.
Always we must separate
Real and unreal. Postulate
Our position and acclaim
Truth in action for the same.

Free Flight

The gulls today are riding on the wind,
Their grace and ease accentuating flight;
Their gliding gives a special turn of thought
That makes me envy them their wingéd right.
The wind is wild, increasing their delight
In oneness with the elements of air.
The rain, that is an obligato strange,
Extends an added zest to their bold range.
And I, indoors, admiring so their skill,
Vicariously swoop with them at will.

Spirit

Because all life is ebb and flow,
A waxing, waning frequency,
It is imperative to know
That spirit is the constancy.

Early Moon

Quite early in the afternoon,
I looked out on our lovely view,
And there I found a special boon;
To my delight, I saw the moon,
Between some clouds right in the blue,
A moon at least three quarter size,
Majestic in its daylight reign.
I looked away then back again;
It somehow caught me by surprise,
There in the sunlight—high moon-rise.
It pleasured me to find it there,
Serene and beautiful, with flair.
It gave the day an added grace,
An extra fillip to embrace.

Our Strength

Communion service at St. Peter's Church–
Or Chapel, really; it is very small–
This morning where I went to praise the Lord,
I offered and presented all myself,
My soul and body as a sacrifice–
A living sacrifice the prayer book says–
Unto the Lord, with all my utmost strength.
It is the closest service of the Church;
By closest meaning nearness to our God.
For when we take the Wafer and the Wine,
As Body and as Blood of Jesus Christ,
He enters us, as we do Him; and thus
We always have a strength from the Divine.
If we could but remember this always,
We'd have a Guide to help us, with such Love,
We'd never fear to act as Christians should.

Vapors

The fog is here in whiteness tipped with gray;
It hovers on the water heavily,
As if to press it down in mental gloom,
Sometimes appearing thick and menacing,
At others, evanescent veils of smoke.
Quite arbitrary in erratic ways,
Enveloping rapaciously at will,
Yet suddenly releasing from its grasp
The ordinary distance of the view.
Capricious, but with undercurrent strong
Of self-determined will and rigidness.
In looking at the bay, it's a white wall
Of vapor just beyond the water line;
A heavy mistiness that permeates
The very atmosphere with awesome urge.
It's very like depression of the mind,
That flounders in its own entangling net,
With inability to look ahead,
Or even look within for guidance true.
A sense of fine proportion is quite lost
With both these strange phenomena at large.
Depression is a fog within the brain,
Creating havoc when it's thickly veiled,
Less dreadful when opacity retires,
And leaves the aura only of the depth
Of dismal gloom the mind sinks down into.
Dejection overcome lets in the light;
So lifting fog reveals the props we know,
And dissipating, leaves horizons clear,
Horizons of the mind with warm delight.

Full Moon and Clouds

The moon is roundly full tonight and clear.
It came up pinkish yellow from the sea,
But now it's silver white and strangely cold.
Its shadow on the water of the bay
Lights up the wavelets rippling into land.
Above the moon itself a blanket shows
Of heavy clouds, the less dense in the van.
Their menace does not figure with her yet,
But presently the lighter wisps declare
Their opalescence with her back of them;
The path of light still shines across the bay.
Then finally the darker clouds take charge,
And quietly the silver way recedes,
But slowly, as with caution, dimming down.
At last there's just a circle further out
That still shows light, as if the Lord stood there.
Then all goes dark, and one can only hear
The slapping of the waves upon the sand.

Success?

Oh, what is then your offer to the world?
Is it yourself, your own ideas, your life?
What have you learned to help you on the way
To make you want to share what you have won?
You seem so sure that others want to know
Your secret of success, your way of life.
Did you assume this knowledge on your own?
And did you glean it as you went along?
Or was there sudden light as with St. Paul?
What is the touchstone of your surety?
Have you gained your own soul in all this quest?
To reap what profit in the earthly mart
Would you consider having feet of clay?
These questions must be asked to get insight,
To know the reasons for the attitudes,
To see things clearly etched within the mind,
Where knowing truth redeems the world with love,
And giving all of self incurs the soul.

Compliance

The wind, a penetrating, sweeping wind,
So strong it tugs the essence of one's stance,
And beautiful as it develops more
In magnitude and rushes at all things
That stand within its reach in awesome fear,
Relinquishing whatever is desired.
So does a wild love in its passion high
Demand one's acquiescence to comply.

Serenity

The very attribute we want the most
Is just the one that cannot be attained
By striving. It must come with ease and calm,
In quietness of mind and heart and soul;
Its name tranquillity. And that we earn
By being undisturbed in all we do,
In everything we think and feel and love.
We have to give ourselves and not hold back;
Relax into the highest that we know,
Accept with grace and strength what comes our way,
Fulfilling with a Christian quietness
The destiny we're given and we mold.
If we can muster what we need for this,
Then we have gained our aim—Serenity.

Christmas

If now the Babe of Bethlehem were born,
How would He find us taking up our time?
In egocentric planning, racial scorn,
Dishonor, desolation, and discord?
With armaments amassing by the score
For war unspeakable? With greed and lust?
With tortures so refined they blur the mind
To contemplate? Man's inhumanity
To man? We are not merely dust, but just
A little lower than the angels are.
Why then do we not covenant to bar
The nameless horrors that abound so far?
The Babe of Bethlehem IS born again
Whenever, in our hearts, we let Him be.
He comes with peace, with joy, good will to men,
To those who fearlessly pursue His Star.

Change

When one is young, the body then obeys;
The mental and the physical enmesh.
But later on the promptings of the mind
Cannot create the same response it did,
And one is sad at first but then accepts
The lessons age should teach to everyone,
That spirit is the essence of our needs,
And we must learn serenity to win
The greatest satisfaction of the soul.

Very Early Spring

I walked along the beach today,
In lovely mid-March brilliancy;
The wind was down, the air was cool,
The sea aglitter in the bay,
Encouraging the minute waves
To whisper low in ecstasy.
The distant hills along the cliffs
Were softly tinted purple pink,
The shoals were tawny, washed in gold.
Such glory gave me pause to think,
To ponder humbly and behold
The generosity of God.
Then nearly home, up on our road,
A butterfly in beauty came.
Its colors were magnificent,
Like lapis-lazuli, within
An edging of a soft écru,
And when the sun shone on it full,
A glint like fired bronze came through.
It was exciting there to see
This fragile creature out of time,
To wonder why it should appear
So strangely early in the year.
It certainly gave untold zest
To me in its erratic quest,
And marked a day already full
Of beauty with its own bequest.

Quiescence

The bay is like a mill pond colored jade,
Periphery of blue and even pink.
There is a quietness defying noise,
That offers compensation to us all.
Serenity pervades the atmosphere,
Demanding reciprocity in man.
Can we accept the challenge and be still,
In order to transform our hecticness
To calm and equal beauty of the soul
And stimulate composure of the mind?

Mutuality

What is the oneness we are aiming for?
Possession is it? Surely that's not right.
Togetherness? Well, partly that, of course.
Reciprocal dependence? In a way.
But mostly it's a love that's unconfined,
With such an understanding each to each,
That all the world acknowledges and sees
The loveliness engendered in its calm
And ever present fearless destiny.

My Sister Fan—1973

Her soul is still imprisoned in her flesh,
Awaiting freedom at the stroke of death.
Her personality is like a mesh
Of emptiness and blank interstices;
A cryptic nothingness of only breath.
No recognition of her loved ones now.
Vacuity has taken precedence.
So do we pray the Lord will soon allow
Her to discard her present human form
And go at last to His own Providence.

Mid-March

The peepers have been singing loud and strong;
They've made me happy with their bell-like song.
For one whole week they've given out their ring
Of joyous welcome, advertising spring.

And now, despite the weather's wind and cold,
When sounds of hylas are not quite so bold,
We know they're ever waiting to embrace
Spring's second upsurge with a happy grace.

Determination is the part they play
Defying winter in a special way.
I love them for their sheer tenacity,
Their prophecy and perspicacity.

I love them for their gentle gaiety
And constant music without satiety,
The friendliness that they seem to create,
And to the loveliness that they relate.

Our World

What is this world we're in? It's physical.
We know it in its actuality–
Our bodies set in all of nature's ways.
But God breathed spirit into man, besides,
And that is what our essence really is.
So when our bodies sicken out at last,
Our souls return to Him from whence they came.
And surely spirit has no color line,
Nor sect, nor sex, nor any of Earth's ways,
But transcends everything that's animal.
Thus showing how absurd it is to carp
On whether God is black or white or, too,
A man or woman or whatever else;
God is a Spirit, as we well should know.
This was explained to us by Jesus when
He came and took on man's humanity.
So why then don't we listen with our ears
And see with eyes that comprehend God's Word?
Man strains at gnats and swallows camels whole,
But one day man will venture into truth,
And then this earth will shine with love and light.

Erosion

Erosion of the shore near which we live
Is evident as storms of magnitude
Flare up in raucous deviltry to give
Progressive seepage. Like a turpitude
That is erosion of a conscience strange
In lacking honor so beyond its range.
What's happened to our morals at this time?
Have they relinquished to desuetude
Their rights and use and strength to evil care?
What catalyst can jog them in repair?
It's obvious that something must be done.
The search for truth has got to be begun,
And faithfully on course it can be won.
When we gain truth, the truth shall make us free.
Our Lord said that, and surely He must know;
He died to prove it, thus it must be so.

A Fillip

How to describe the greyness of the sea?
The slaty look it has, the flatness, too.
Like tiles to roof a large chateau in France?
Or battleships in harbor, motionless?
A pencil line of pink injects itself
Between the water and the darker sky;
A sky that's bruised near the horizon's edge,
Then pales into a dome of sooty white.
To put this into words is difficult;
The total ambiance though quite subdued,
Evokes with just that linear design,
Encouragement to overcome a fate
Of dull depression in the atmosphere.
So always with a monotone of tasks,
One fillip creates joy that supersedes.

Questing

O, let me write a poem that is full
Of love and beauty and the spirit's truth,
With universal knowledge that reflects
In sympathy on old age and on youth,
Assuring them in all simplicity
A meeting ground of faith's felicity.
Inviting both to rise and join the quest
For searching out life's meaning at its best,
And with the special findings then invest
The total wonderful discovery
To God whose Wisdom will assume the rest.

Lustrous Day

First day of autumn,
Glorious day;
Golden and glittering
Diamond-like bay.
Brilliant effusion,
Water and air,
Dancing mobility,
Beauty declare.
Watching delightedly,
Pondering grace,
Indigo skyway
Clouds won't efface.
Sibilant soundings
Down at the beach,
Offer soft murmurings
To the heart's reach.
Gratitude fills me,
Love stretches wide,
Transcendent loveliness
Now acts as guide.

Time Off

I have a thousand things to do today,
But I won't do a single one of them.
Instead, I'll take in beauty by the hour,
Enjoying a fantastic grand display
Of light and shadow frolicking at ease
In chiaroscuro fashion with the breeze.
I'll watch the dogwood blossoms on our tree
In timid shyness flutter graciously,
Above the multi-colored pansies' heads,
Whose velvet softness seems to acquiesce
In gaiety, as singing winds possess
Them with a wildness yet a soft caress.
I'll look out to the sea in eagerness
And view the riffling of the water's way
Meandering delightedly close by,
The gulls dip with a brightness on their wings,
In demonstrating ease of flight, and why
Man emulates such fascinating things.
And see some fishing boats far down the bay,
Their tininess a triumph of command;
Then watch some stratus clouds that seem to lend
Their picturesqueness to the sky's demand.
I survey all this graciousness and spend
Some time in contemplating beauty's theme;
I lose myself but know I understand
The glow and glory of a conscious dream.

Violation — 1975

To me it's inconceivable
That in the world assembly
An anti-Zion vote has won
Approval unbelievable.
Is it not time then for us all
To rise in indignation
And show the world, in strong support,
Our true determination?
It is immoral NOT to speak,
To stand up and be counted,
We must offset this racist hate,
This devious explosion
Of votes that sycophants betrayed
Now causing such erosion.
Let's fight against deceits and lies,
Let's overcome frustrations,
Our world cannot go forward with
A Disunited Nations.

Refugees

What do we know of being dispossessed?
The thirst, the hunger, and the lack of rest?
Old people trying hard to keep the pace,
A child all bloodied on its hands and face;
The heat, the stench, the ghastly look of fear.
The horror of the enemy so near?
The racing heart in terror, on the run,
Increasing suffering that's just begun?
How can the rest of us learn to equate
The dreadfulness of lives in such a state?
At least we can attempt to understand
The tragic loneliness, the desperate stand;
From pictures and descriptions we can see
The anguish and the shocking agony.
May they, in some way, cope with this distress,
Its depth, at which we here can only guess.
The sadness, the incredibility,
Reveals to us such inhumanity,
It is an act of faith to contemplate;
We must through love and strength now compensate.
So let us, then, bow down and pray for peace,
And from this haunting menace man release.

Regeneration

It's Easter; it's the time we should renew
Our inner selves, to strengthen confidence,
To promise silently a solemn vow
To be more Christian in our acts and thoughts.
Somehow, man seems to shun simplicity,
To complicate the workings of his mind,
When all that matters is to clarify
And not make complex all the basic truths.
For God gives evidence of things not seen,
If we'd but hearken with our souls and hearts.
On Easter day our Lord rose from the dead–
The most exciting happening we know;
The Resurrection that gives all of us
The chance to follow Him eternally.
Accepting this in all its mystery,
Rejoicing in the power of its depth;
Let's not forget what has been offered us,
But realize it gratefully with love.

Spaceship Earth

And still the news comes over loud and clear—
The inhumanity of man to man.
How is it when we're given so much here
We try to hurt each other all we can?
So much, it seems to me, is pride and fear,
And putting into diabolic plan,
The longing for such grasping power so sheer
We lose all track of glory that began
When God gave us this Spaceship Earth to span
And meld into a universal sphere.

A Game of Checkers

The two old fellows sat in rapt delight,
Considering the next move of the game;
Their heads were low to make sure they were right
In where they moved their men and what their claim.
The T.V. room of the Old People's Home
Was their arena, no one else was near
To interrupt them. One was like a gnome,
The other huskier—deaf in one ear.
Their concentration was formidable,
As time flowed on, and not a sound was heard.
Then softly, like dry leaves expendable,
A withered hand approached just like a bird
And slowly jumped and took the other's man,
With a triumphant look and crooked smile.
The other never moved, but his eyes ran
Around the situation, and with guile
He jumped two men and laughed in outright glee;
For his opponent only one remained,
And he was very sure that he had three,
Which should give him the win, though he refrained
From gloating outwardly, he clutched his cane
And held it tight in inward happiness,
Awaiting salutation's glad refrain
To fill his cup of joy and wizardry.

January Jinks

Zero weather, sunlight brilliance,
Snow and ice and special clouds,
Breath exhaled is smoke for seconds,
Breath inhaled brings peppermint.
Joyous January high jinks
Gives surprises and delight,
Makes us realize caprices,
Whims of nature and her strength.
Ice with snow has filled the bay front,
Freezing it to cobalt hue,
Touching off prismatic lightings,
Sparkling xanthene verities.

Eclipse—May 30th, 1984

Ancients said,
In times gone by,
That eclipses
Are to show
Sun and Moon
Do integrate
To examine
And discuss
Situations
On our Earth.
Now I wonder
What today
Sun and Moon
In their own way
Have discovered
Of much mirth.

Solitude

If loneliness is being by one's self,
Then I am lonely.
But by myself I have a lovely time,
For in reality I'm not alone;
I'm working, reading, contemplating rhyme,
Enjoying all the beauty I am prone
To, with a heart that dances in delight
For all the loveliness within its sight,
And joy in true accomplishment for me,
With wondrous thoughts that keep me company.
I am not lonely,
For by myself I have a lovely time.

Submission

As clouds must be submissive to the wind,
So loyal Christians must obey the Lord.
Not in a sequence of passivity,
But in an act of Love proposed by God,
And inwardly accepted thus by man.
In activating this procedure free,
Results promote a faithfulness so true,
The glory of its light ignites the soul.

Young Moon

O, such a young moon in the sky last night;
It looked so tremulous yet sure of life,
A lighted crescent waxing in the vault
Of heaven, tenuous but strong.
And Venus lending credence to the scene,
Inviting friendship with its nearness there,
While adding to the beauty of the dark,
The velvet atmosphere in backdrop sheer.
And in the east there still was afterglow
Enclosing clouds in an unusual pink,
Which lasted only seconds as I watched.
The beauty that we see intensifies
The sadnesses we feel within our hearts,
Yet at the same time offers us relief—
An easing of our sorrows with its grace.

Development

Time takes its toll,
Of that we know;
But if we're wise,
Attempting grace,
Our spirits grow.

Interim

The beauty of today demands our praise
For something perfect and incredible.
The calmness of the water and the air
Gives a serenity that offers trust,
A cloudless sky invokes the spirit's calm,
The brilliancy of light illuminates
Each thing it touches with a clarity
So pure one wonders if it can be real.
The sunlight on the lawn is more than bright
Against the shadows of the nearby trees,
While on the water of the cobalt bay
There's only a susurrus sound to hear.
It's like a time between two other times,
When man must stop to take a truthful look
At what is happening and where he is,
And in the effort of distinguishing
He is rewarded with the ideal way.

Sorrow

Grief makes a complex mixture in the heart,
Erratic as the sun and rain of spring,
Creating variables in approach
To life and how to cope with it alone.
At times there is a strengthening within,
Enabling one to manage easily,
At others there's a vacuum to breach
In order just to keep above the flood
Of sensed defeat and lonelinesss combined.
One battles on, in knowledge that in time
The faith that carried so far will obtain
In all the days remaining on this earth,
And show the substance that is hoped for now
In evidence unseen but fully known,
With understanding and serenity
Transcending separateness to unity.

Monotone

The wind is howling all around the house,
With snow in drifts in special places where
It always goes in storms as strong as this.
And for a ways one sees the snow-topped ice
That joins the bay in threatened jeopardy.
But one can't see too far because of snow
In flying, looping, wild-like freeziness,
And everything is white and grey and cold;
A painting that's an artist's monotone.

Vigilant

A watchful time to one who waits for grace,
For patience to accept the things that are,
In knowing that the trust behind what is
Must soon give evidence of all to be.
It seems a lengthy time to contemplate,
To offer everything that one holds close,
But one remembers what is sacrifice
And quietly enfolds the soul within.

Venture

The vault of sky is blue beyond compare,
Enticing swimming in it with the soul,
And diving through the brilliancy that's there
With such delight it merits its own goal.
Let's surge through timelessness and space and light
With such abandon of our spirits' care
We'll feel the gracefulness of special flight,
And know in depth the basic art to dare.

Communion

I went to church this morning
The wind was riding high,
It gave me thoughts to ponder
Of where it goes and why.
For it is like the spirit,
As Jesus told us when
He used it in comparison:
The wind—the souls of men.
From whence it comes, and where it goes
We hear the sound thereof
But cannot know the answer,
Except that it is love.
So when I took Communion,
To God I offered me,
My soul, my body, everything,
With love that made me free.

Light-ness

There were a myriad of stars last night;
I went out on the deck to watch from there.
The first one I could see was Jupiter,
Fantastic in its brightness in the east,
And then, as I grew more accustomed to
The night around me, I saw stars abound.
It was magnificent, a sheer display
Of light and glory in the vault of sky.
Primarily I'd been alert to view
The moon-rise from the water of the bay,
But clouds, low-lying, made the rise come late,
Which gave me some more time to watch the stars.
And then a pinkness showed above the sea;
A pink and golden ball displaced the black
Of the horizon and gave forth its lure,
Entrancing me as I stood looking out,
Enabling me to put all loneliness
Inside the light-ness of this special night.

Living

In giving, sometimes taking, we must live,
To bear, forbear, and always to forgive,
To have regard for all things that we are
But more of what we try to be, the star
Of our delight and comfort to uphold
Our love and faith and hopefulness untold.
We must be sure to gather patience in,
To learn to live anew, and to begin
To love above all else, within our span,
The Grace of God, the sanctity of man.

Progression

The gulls can ride the wind,
But I a whirlwind ride,
Progressing in a swirl
To empty passive thought,
Then get a safer stride
Of positivity.
The calmness of the mind
Requires active grace,
Acceptance with accord
And equanimity,
So off the whirlwind goes,
While I seek safer pace;
I simulate the gulls
Incorporating space.

Directions

In living day to day, as we *should* do,
We learn to know the ever-present Now.
We don't affront the future with our fears,
Nor worry back the past in sad regret;
We live right in the moment of our lives.
In doing this we grasp a special fact:
The Omnipresent is Infinity.
This is exciting knowledge for the soul,
Enabling us to see and act the truth,
Allowing us relinquishment of power
That is more powerful when we agree
To let the Lord control our lives not us,
Yet doing what we sense He means us to,
Admitting His complete authority,
While offering, with grace and joy, our wills
To Him Who then directs our every path.

Summer Sonnet

It is a lovely day and very fair;
There is a breeze that sweeps across the bay,
A riffling of the water on display
As it creates a coolness in the air.
It lends the heart rejection of despair,
Inviting joy to partner it in play,
To take on heights of freedom without care
And join the lustrousness with no delay.
It is a happiness quite all its own;
As, relegating worries to their place,
It adds a fillip to its graceful tone
And captures nuances of faith, to face
The troubled times we pray will not arrive,
But which are possible to all alive.

Warning of the Wind

O Wind, what are you telling us?
You've been exhorting mightily
All winter and now more in spring.
Some secret message is within
The loudness of your voice, a ring
That seems to warn us of much sin
And what we're doing in this world.
If we could listen with our hearts
Perhaps we'd know the reason why
You take the trouble to incite
Our thinking for a plan that's right
In exercising bold restraint
From nuclear destruction here.
And when you speak less noisily,
Your modulation still brings fear.
The message that you gave before
Remains the same in quietness:
"Take care, you worldlings, of this place,
Do not destroy the human race."

Symbiosis

As he and she are so much one,
Their thoughts and tastes are now that way;
Ideas similar are run
Between their minds in fine array.
As fungus is to alga part,
A secret mirror to possess,
These two know deep each other's heart,
To their delight and happiness.
As lichen they're each other's strength,
In harmony, as man and wife.
And, as their years draw on in length,
They fortify each other's life.
In perfect symbiosis, they
Reflect a lovely unity,
Establishing in every way
Their love into infinity.

Offering

What a lovely way
To spend a day,
Thinking of others
And what they may
Need to get through.
With some this comes naturally,
Others need specificity
In knowing what to do.
And with just a few,
Intuition rings true:
So, love is offered
From me to you.

Meteorite—March 1983

A rock from Mars, the physicists announce,
Is here on Earth. What news that does pronounce!
But how it got here is the question mark,
At least as well as I can understand.
But they will work it out I have no doubt,
They seem to know what it is all about,
If not the full logistics of the trip.
How fascinating just to contemplate,
In daring to assume and correlate
The facts as they are given us to know.
It offers possibilities to grow
A whole new concept of a Martian world
Of extra-terra life that could be real,
As Sagan sometimes offers with appeal.
I get great pleasure thinking this is true,
As in God's house so many mansions thrive,
Inhabitants, perforce, must be alive.

Summer—1978

The lovely days this summer were so few
That when they came they offered such delight
One almost held one's breath in ecstasy.
Then all the dampness and the fog and wet
Were quite forgotten in excessive joy;
The light that was so unbelievable
In its distinctness and its flashing grace,
Creating gemlike glittering displays;
The grandeur of the clouds of cumulus
Traversing in majestic guise the sky;
The water of the bay and sea so blue
It made a lapis pool in which to leap.
The distance one could see seemed infinite,
And in one's soul one knew that this was true,
As all this beauty, in its rarity,
Invoked response with gratitude and love.

Blame

Why is there cancer?
Why is there pain?
Why is there cruelty
Hunger and war?
Doesn't God care?
Are we alone?
Are we just animals
Loving our own?
That's what it seems like
Right at this time.
But deep down within us,
Surely we know
That God is with us,
Trying to show
That man is the enemy
All to himself,
Creating illness,
Havoc and death.
God gave us free will;
That's where we sin,
Taking a wrong road
Then blaming Him.
Let us remember
The best way we can:
God gave Himself
To redeem man.

Twilight

It's getting dark, the gulls are homeward bound;
They ride the wind in a tumultuous sky,
In silence and in freedom, with no fear.
There's nothing tremulous or tentative
In their instinctive natural return.
I watch in wonder at their facileness
And wish that I could emulate their grace,
As I look out and ponder until dark.

Outlook

Atop a sandcliff is my lovely home,
A view that's unsurpassed looks out to sea,
With first the bay and then the island's reach,
Another island to the left oblique.
It is a thrilling place to live for me;
I love the changes of the seasons here—
Including winter with its icy spell—
A challenge in such variable ways.
Experience of moonrise is unique,
It is enchantment and felicity,
With such a feeling of infinity
It offers oneness with the universe.

Accountability

The things that are impossible with man,
Are possible with God, as we should know,
So therefore let us pray, expecting strength
To fortify us when we need much help.
We need it now, when Armageddon lurks
In readiness to strike upon our earth.
The world must jettison all atom bombs,
For nuclear destruction is too close;
The vast decisive conflict shall be waged
With words and understanding, faith and hope,
Not weapons scorching mankind to the death.
We can and shall excel in peace, not war.
For man must realize it's up to him
To be responsible for what he has,
To make this world a place where all must live
In peace and love and the Almighty's Grace.

The Cardinal

The day was dark;
The sky so gray
It seemed as though
We'd get more snow.
Or rain, at least.
The air was damp,
The wind was high.
The atmosphere
A sense of fear.
As if a strange
And awesome sight
Might soon appear.
But suddenly
A bright streak flashed
Above the tree
That was near me.
A cardinal
In his array
Of lovely red
Gave out his call.
Nor was that all;
His mate arrived
As he desired.
Together they
In keen relay
Both gave to me
A brilliancy.
And so it is

In this strange world.
We never know
How things will go,
Because a change
Beyond our range
Makes magic glow.

Thankfulness

I went down to the water's edge and felt
The lovely coldness of the constant sea
And thought its unique motion and its cool
Would confidently give serenity.
The pebbles I picked up and washed, all seemed
To have a quietness and clarity
That gave me joy and wonder in my heart,
And so I washed my thoughts as well, to see
How free of fear they could become when cleansed,
And got assurance of tranquillity.
It seemed incredible that I should find
A quietude and calm so easily.
But then I realized that everything
Is made to shape into our destiny.
If we can understand, appreciate
The gift of love from The Divinity.
Thus this Thanksgiving Day I thank the Lord
For all the loveliness and beauty here
And wait for the unfolding Grace to come
In patience 'til the time it shall appear.

A Small Star

Fetch me a little star, O heart,
That I can hitch my wagon to,
Give my ideas a running start
For ideals worthy to construe.
Simplify complications' weave,
Unknotting rough entanglements,
Creating credos to believe,
Jettisoning all impediments.
Gently ease my mind's constructions
Into a true reality,
Let there be no rough obstructions
To curb the soul's fidelity.

Sunset Light

The fishtraps give out light at sunset time
That is a colorful and silent rhyme,
In such a poem as is beautiful,
With undercurrents that are mystical.
It is ephemeral, so maybe why
There is a poignancy involved to try
To understand the mystery involved.
Then suddenly the questing is resolved;
The light has changed, the traps are now mundane,
Which gives out answers that are true and plain:
In everything and everyone with light,
There is created a unique delight.

Windows on the World

And now I've seen the Windows on the World
Atop the World Trade Center in New York.
It's so incredible I can't believe
The vastness of the view I saw that night;
The grandeur of the lights for miles around,
With diamond bracelet bridges crossing to
Long Island and New Jersey and the Bronx.
It made me gasp in unbelief to see
Incredulous perspective realized.
And then, on looking up into the sky,
I noted with delight a lustrous moon,
As serendipity gave me a nudge.
When peering south I saw the statue there
Of Liberty, with torch lit up to show
A new home still to those who wish to come.
And as I gazed upon such magicness
Of lights and coruscation all around,
I thought how great man can be when he tries,
Attempting grandness in his skyward climb,
And in creativeness to beauty rise.

Capability

To walk in space is what man's done
In nineteen hundred eighty-four.
Big Brother not responsible,
In spite of Orwell's prophecy
Of man a cog within the state.
The thought of such accomplishment
Is so exciting to the mind,
It makes one proud to be a part
Of what is known as humankind.
But in the world the wars go on,
And mostly they're religious wars.
It makes one shudder just to know
How schizophrenia world peace mars;
We have to prove duality
Of human nature can be checked,
To curb the baseness of the one
And raise the other to the stars.

Sonnet

O, let us never be afraid to live,
But act with courage, and share love always.
Not casting doubt on truth when sin betrays,
But try to sublimate ourselves and give
A sympathetic heart that's sensitive,
Assuring others with its true displays
What we are sure the very soul portrays,
While ever cherishing the positive.
O, let us truly stand up straight and tall.
Be counted, with no doubts, for charity,
That other name for love. As we recall
Our deepest thoughts with clarity;
Engaging in the strength to understand
The human needs we share at love's command.

Soul's Perspective

Beauty all about us—
But many people sick.
How does one equate it?
And how does it relate?
The angel at Bethesda
Could handle this in stride;
The empathy within him
Enabled him to guide
The startling mixed emotions
But separated fine,
With each its own perspective,
The human and divine.
So loveliness gives strength
To handle and accept
The tragedies and happiness
Involved in man's concept.

Restorative

All those who love have special graciousness;
Their world is full of understanding, joy,
Their attitude creates an ambiance
Of happiness that evermore responds,
Of quiet effervescence that pervades
The very sanctuary of the heart.
Their presence recreates its own rewards,
As when it offers some small part of them,
Refreshing others with their golden love.

Effort

To love mankind is easy,
More or less;
But to love one's neighbor—
Not mention like—
Gives guiltiness
For not attempting it,
Not even with finesse.

Moon Frame

The sky last night was lit with a full moon,
Which came through clouds of mackerel design
That periscoped in ripples of soft light
In framing this earth's only satellite–
In watching it I gave a prayer of thanks
For startling beauty in a world its own,
While giving us a key to secret paths.

Share with Love

The pictures of the starving Africans
Are so horrific it is hard to look.
With so much extra food in granaries
In these United States it makes one stop
In shock and pain at such inequities
Existing in this world of ours today.
What can be done is starting to be done
At last, but meanwhile thousands more are dead.
This topsy-turvy planet in its flight
Through space, must gear itself to fight right on
And share with love what every man must have.

Complacency

Sometimes we are so full of self
That we don't realize
Stupidity is mirrored in
Our egocentric eyes.
It's then we should look carefully,
To contemplate our sins
And turn our selfishness around
Where reaching out begins.

Disparity

Morning sunlight
Highwayed the ocean.
While darkening clouds
Precluded sunfall
On the gloom-set bay.
The sea however,
Gave such enchantment
With its swath of light,
I felt excitement
Just watching it play.
Illumination
Upon the ocean,
Greyness on the bay,
Gave significance
And variation
To life's differing
And impartial way.

Faith

Rejoice and be of hopeful mind,
Take heart in knowing we can find
The strength to cope with what life metes
By praying hard. Nothing defeats
The spirit that's inborn and true,
As darkness lets the light come through.
An axiom to bear in thought
Is knowing sin by love is bought.
And when we cannot see our way,
We learn by faith the path to stay,
With unseen power in supply,
Our hearts uplifted, heads held high.

JANE BALDWIN GILLESPIE

Poet and teacher, Jane Baldwin Gillespie has drawn much of the inspiration for *Susurrus,* her second published collection of poems, from the surroundings of her home overlooking Gardiner's Bay on outer Long Island. She retired to East Hampton in 1971 after an active life in education and raising her family. Her first book, *Making Melody,* was enthusiastically received in 1983, and she has recently resumed teaching as a member of Literacy Volunteers of Suffolk County.

A native of New York, she was graduated from Miss Porter's School in Farmington, Conn., took courses at Columbia University, and later Mt. Holyoke College where she trained in the treatment of reading disorders. She taught the fourth grade for many years at the Hill School, a country day school in Middleburg, Virginia, where her husband, the late C. Waring Gillespie was headmaster. She also tutored children with dyslexia at the Eaglebrook School, Deerfield, Mass., and at the Greenwich Country Day School, Greenwich, Conn.

Mrs. Gillespie worked at the *Reader's Digest* and for several years ran a small shop in Mt. Kisco, New York, where she grew up and where she and her husband lived and brought up their two daughters. She has also traveled extensively in Europe and Great Britain.